Recollections from My Time in the Indian Service 1935 - 1943

Maria Martinez Makes Pottery

ISBN 0-9651377-1-6

Cover painting *Santo Domingo Cermonial Dance* by Alfreda Ward Maloof.
Back cover photograph of the author by Kathryn G. Maloof.

Book design and compilation by Living Gold Press, Jill Livingston and Kathryn Golden Maloof.

All pottery designs depicted in this book are of Santo Domingo or San Ildefonso origin.

Printed on recycled paper.

Recollections from My Time in the Indian Service 1935 -1943

including my primer
Maria Martinez Makes Pottery

Alfreda Ward Maloof

LIVING GOLD PRESS

This book is lovingly dedicated
To all my Indian friends in Arizona + New Mexico
and the Great Northern Plains
especially Those
in the Pueblos of Santo Domingo + San Ildefonso
for whom I still have fond memories after 60 years.

Alta Loma, California March 1997

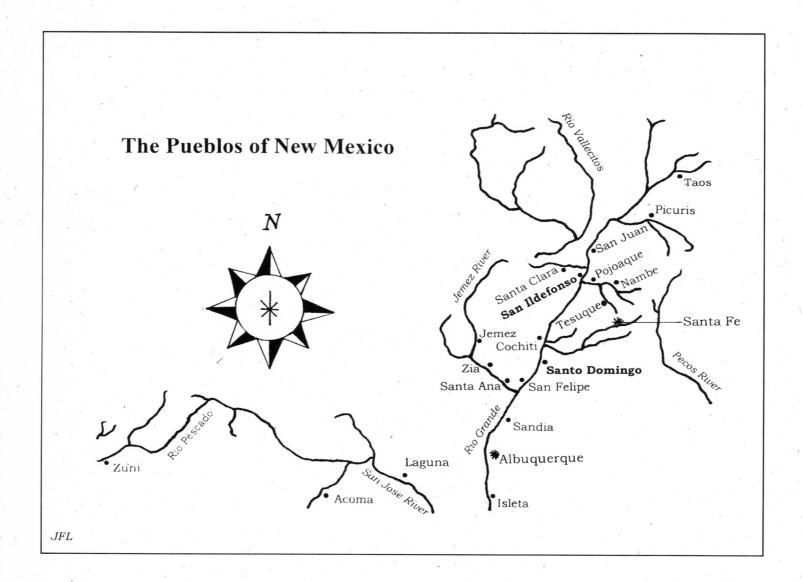

The Pueblos of New Mexico

N

Rio Vallecitos

Taos

Picuris

San Juan

Pojoaque

Santa Clara

Nambe

San Ildefonso

Jemez River

Tesuque

Santa Fe

Jemez

Cochiti

Pecos River

Zia

Santo Domingo

Santa Ana

San Felipe

Rio Grande

Sandia

Rio Pescado

Albuquerque

Laguna

Zuni

San Jose River

Acoma

Isleta

JFL

I awoke from out of the darkness into a strange new world on that cool February dawn. As the sunrise began to penetrate the tall, narrow window, I arose to peek out at the slowly awakening village across the way, to try to imagine what my time in this alien place might bring. Everything around me was brown. The village walls were brown, the people were brown, the ground was brown...so different from the subtropical well-irrigated Southern California from where I'd come. A little scared, I felt like I was at the end of the world, but not wholly unpleasant. The tiny knot of apprehension in my stomach quickly turned to hunger thanks to the drifting smells of baking bread. Taking in the varied sensations, my groggy brain began to clear. I was able to trace the enticing odor to the tray of crusty loaves being pulled from the round clay oven that sat on the hard packed ground of someone's back yard. The baker, a woman with long dark hair tied behind her head and a striped woolen blanket draped about her shoulders, disappeared into a square flat-roofed adobe home. A small herd of goats tussled among themselves as the sun gained strength. The crow of a rooster and yip of a dog broke my reverie....So much to do! Only two days to prepare for school!

The solitary journey away from the bosom of my family and into what seemed to me a barren, open land had begun forty eight hours earlier. I stepped off the platform at the depot in Pomona, California and onto an eastbound train, heading for Albuquerque, New Mexico. At last I had found a job befitting my education. I had graduated from UCLA with a teaching degree. I also had a keen interest in studying art, but money for necessary art materials was hard to come by due to the Depression. So I settled on teaching. In the summer of 1934, I was a hopeful but frustrated graduate wondering down what paths life would take me. But the immediate concern of Alfreda Ward that summer was a JOB.

I had never ventured far from my home in LaVerne, California, although my mother was a native of Sweden and my father of English descent. I searched far and wide for a teaching job that summer to no avail. In desperation I took a job selling candy at a five and dime near my home. A menial job that taught me about salesmanship, something that would be useful later. Little did I know that a routine trip to the post office would change the course of my life.

Standing in line to buy stamps, I noticed the circular from the U.S. Department of Interior, Bureau of Indian Affairs posted on the wall. It seems they were looking for someone to teach second and third grades at Santo Domingo, a Pueblo village in New Mexico. What did I have to lose? I desperately needed a good job, teaching was my chosen profession, I was ready for anything.

I duly applied for the job. After months of mailbox watching I had heard nothing, so I took it upon myself to write to Washington. In reply I received a surly telegram informing me that "the government will work in its own good time." That was very discouraging! But to my surprise it wasn't long before I received yet another telegram, this one telling me to report to Santo Domingo. My salary was to be $1640 a year. Sixty years later, the memories of my life there in New Mexico, in what at first seemed like a foreign land, are still fresh and stimulating.

In my new smock, a gift from home

The train arrived in Albuquerque at dusk. I was to report to the Indian Office there for further instructions. I felt a little lost, but confident. A handsome Navajo was to take me the rest of the way to Santo Domingo by car. Well after dark, he left me with Miss Nori, the school principal. She led me to one of the houses in the teachers' quarters, the only wooden structure in the village. It was actually just outside the village proper, right next to the flat roofed adobe school house. I had reached my new home, Santo Domingo Pueblo. I resolved to get a good nights sleep.

As I was soon to learn, Santo Domingo is one of nineteen pueblos in New Mexico, the Rio Grande Pueblos. Each pueblo has its own identity and own Indian government. There were some differences in dress and hairstyles. The pueblos did not all share the same ancient language. Santo Domingo is one of the "southern" pueblos, meaning it is south of Santa Fe, and the native language is called Kerasan. It is a quiet language and seems to originate down in the throat.

The Indians we have come to collectively call "Pueblo Indians" are actually scattered groups of people living within a certain geographical area. The many pueblos have varied but similar traditions, religions, economics, languages. The native people in this part of New Mexico have all lived under the dominance of three foreign governments, the Spanish, the Mexican, and the United States. The Hispanic influence is obvious, as seen in the name of my new home and the names of many of my new students and neighbors. The Pueblo Indians of the 1930s spoke a mixture of their native tongues, Spanish, and English.

The Pueblo Indians remarkably have retained their own identities in spite of so much outside influence. Each pueblo has its Catholic church, but the ancient religion has meshed neatly with the Catholic religion. The traditional dances and ceremonies are still practiced, often in conjunction with a Catholic Saint's day. And unlike many other Native Americans, the Pueblo Indians are fortunate to still reside in the same localities in which they were first discovered by invading Europeans, although of course their villages are now known by their Hispanic names rather than the ancient Indian names. The pueblo of Santo Domingo as it is known today originated from a 75,000 acre land grant given to the Indians by the Spanish crown in 1689, later confirmed by an act of Congress in 1858.

But on my arrival at Santo Domingo I was only vaguely aware of all this. My immediate concern was to settle into my new home and prepare for the start of my teaching career as "Miss Ward" (or "Meese Warts", as the children said my name). My house mate was another teacher, Miss Paceley. She came from Indiana and her little dog MacNut, that she loved to distraction, was named after the Governor of her home state. The other teachers were Miss Perry who came from Georgia and Miss Driskell from North Dakota. We four were the only non-Indians in Santo Domingo.

Miss Nori was the principal. She was an Indian from the Laguna Pueblo. The thirties were more formal times to be sure, but given our close quarters and common purpose, I soon came to call them Elsie, Reba, Elizabeth, and Verna.

I had only a day or two to arrange my things, bring in a supply of coal for heat, plan my lessons, and explore the village a little bit. It was only the end of February, but I watched the men plowing their fields and planting corn, the crop that has been at the foundation of my new neighbor's civilization for centuries.

With little time to reflect on things, I began to teach. It was a basic "three Rs" type of education. But our course of study included some things that I'm sure weren't included in lesson plans back home in California. Hygiene and water supply were quite primitive in the village. The source of clean water

Myself, Miss Perry, Monica Silva, Miss Nori, Miss Paceley, Miss Driskell

was the well up near the school, from which the villagers carried their supplies in buckets. Many of the children had infrequent opportunities to wash at home. So the first thing each school morning the children washed, combed their hair (always on the lookout for lice, another of our responsibilities), and brushed their teeth. Monica Silva, a Santa Clara Indian married to a Santo Domingan, was in charge of this health program. We took care of simpler health problems such as eye and ear infections and delousing. A nurse came by now and then. In those pre-antibiotic days, the village had its share of disease, including T.B., syphilis, typhoid. We served cod-liver oil to the under-nourished.

Reyes Quintana and Monica Silva

Reyes Quintana was another school employee. He served as both a handyman and a truant officer and disciplinarian. He would go to the homes of absent children to find out why they weren't in school that day. Ever so often he would send me from the room and give the class a big lecture. I never found out what they were about. I found I was shut out of or just plain ignorant of many things going on around me. In almost all matters the Indian Governor of the Pueblo and his Council had jurisdiction. Reyes was an intermediary and saw to most of the necessary discipline that was beyond my scope.

The Council got after the children for letting the white teachers hear and learn Indian words. But this was inevitable since many of the younger students knew very little English, and they also enjoyed sharing their language with us. Village rules were that after crossing the irrigation ditch on the way to school, only English could be spoken. The reverse was true on the way home.

On the other hand, Indian assimilation into Anglo culture was the goal of the Indian Service until two or three decades later. There was also a disturbing faction of the Bureau of Indian Affairs that thought teaching the Indians was a waste of time for most would eventually just "go back to the blanket," as the saying went. These deeper issues were disturbing, but mostly I kept my thoughts on the job that I was hired to do—to give the children their basic building blocks of an education and look out for their physical well-being.

The kids were mostly sweet and eager to learn. I got along well with Pedro but he could be a real trouble maker. I hadn't been teaching more than two weeks when I lost my temper, shook him hard and ripped his shirt. Was I ever ashamed. I had to keep him in at recess so I could mend his shirt! I needed to repair not only the rip in the fabric but also the tear in our teacher/student relationship. I'm glad I had just one Pedro in my class.

I sent Antonio home one day for misbehaving. He thought I meant he was to stay home for good, was very upset and went crying to Reyes. Many times a misbehaving student had to spend the bulk of the school day sitting on the floor in the corner. One day the children were all more or less "drunk" on chewing tobacco, girls and boys alike, and some of them plenty sick. Another time, they might play a game of throwing cockleburs in each others hair, and what a chore it was to get the burrs out without taking half a head of hair with them. And it could be distracting the way they'd eat pine nuts in the classroom when I was trying to give a lesson. They'd pop them in one side of their mouths and spit the shells out the other side onto the floor. In one side and out the other, all day long. They did the same thing with cottonwood blossoms. Every day they seemed to think up some new clever trick.

Still, Pedro or one of the others never failed to show up at my house after school to bring in coal or do other light chores in exchange for a cookie or some other morsel of food. The little girls would come to visit, too. Estella, Delores, and Pasquelita had me fix their hair "like American girls" some afternoons.

I loved the children with their open friendly faces. Teaching in my own classroom was a challenge yet rewarding. I was learning as I went along. I discovered the students had more patience with their lessons if I broke the tedium with little expeditions around the area. Our first trip was through the village to the Rio Grande River. It seemed the entire population watched our procession through the village from their roofs. MacNut came along, of course, and we were joined by several other dogs. We played in the water and posed for pictures on the one-log-wide foot bridge. MacNut fell off and got mud in his eye. Other times we would hike to the hills and dig wild garlic to bring back, do some gardening around the school yard, or plant trees.

Living in a small village of a few hundred people meant that I would naturally come to know many of the students' parents and other adults as well. Although more reticent at first than most people with whom I was familiar, quiet but friendly, I was always made welcome. Many evenings one or another of the fathers would show up at the house for me to read them a letter they had received and sometimes to write one. I wrote a letter to the railroad for Petacio to make a claim for two of his horses run over by the train. I wrote a letter for Asencio ordering a half dozen celluloid drinking cups. Really, their wants and needs were so simple and basic.

Tree trunk bridge over the Rio Grande

Sometimes one of the villagers would come up with items to sell, such as pottery or bows and arrows. Once Pedro's brother wanted to sell me a silver belt for eight dollars to help out his friend whose daughter had died just that morning. As much as I longed to, I could seldom afford to buy any of the beautiful things since I was sending much of my paycheck home as well as saving for a planned trip to Sweden with my mother. On trips to Santa Fe or Albuquerque I confined my purchases to groceries and the occasional movie, only admiring the pottery, blankets, and other wares being sold by Indians set up along side the highway and in town. They would hold up the pots, beckoning to the people passing by, saying "Pottery, pottery?" in high-pitched, singsong voices.

Besides my school work, I had plenty to do. It took a fair amount of time given the primitive conditions to do my washing and cleaning and other house work. My water came out of a hand pump at the sink. I did laundry in a washtub outside. I

Dolores and Estella with siblings - my so very much good helpers

cooked on a coal stove and oil lamps provided light. The attic was full of bats. As the teacher, I was even responsible for cleaning my classroom.

The weather in Santo Domingo kept me guessing. One day it might be hot and summer like, a couple of days later it might snow, then we might have a big wind and dust storm. The wind was the worst! When it would finally stop after several relentless days, it would take me hours to clean the dust and sand and dirt out of my house. The windy weather had the added feature of seeming to whip the local population into an excited state. The kids were wild at school, the parents were wild at home until the wind ceased.

My life was busy and full, but how I missed home and family. In my early days in Santo Domingo, I just about lived for the mail. I got frequent letters from my parents, my sisters, my college and church friends...but not frequent enough. The mail was delivered to what was known as the town of Domingo located a bumpy mile or so away down a sandy road that was almost impassable after a rain. This is where the train station was as well as the Bernalillo Mercantile Store where the Indians bought the groceries they didn't grow for themselves. The two young Mexican fellows that owned the store were always cordial and friendly. They also took Indian jewelry, rugs, and pottery in trade for needed items. I would make the round trip to Domingo daily in about an hour and a half on foot if no one had driven in to collect the mail, hiking over to the tracks and then along them and into the town. The biggest thrill was receiving a package from home chock full of Southern

California treats such as oranges, figs, dates, prunes, jam, avocados. Once they even sent me a dozen eggs. Seven of them arrived intact and along with the other goodies were part of a scrumptious Easter Sunday brunch I shared with the other teachers that year.

A very persistent car salesman had been pestering Miss Paceley to buy a car. I hoped she would make the purchase, as it seemed that it might bring greater mobility to myself as well. Thoughts of sightseeing trips around the area entered my head. The Indian Service occasionally arranged bus expeditions to various places of interest for the teachers from all of the pueblos. But having a car close at hand would make more spontaneous trips possible. I did not always like to spend my weekends in town as the others did—I enjoyed quiet weekends at home and visiting friends in the village—but it would be nice to get into church more regularly or take drives in the mountains.

After a couple of months of negotiating Miss Paceley finally did make her purchase. The salesman delivered it to our house and it looked so elegant. We had some adventures in that car! Of course we got stuck in the sand countless times and had to walk for help. One time we went on a trip to Taos Pueblo and then to see an old out-of-the-way church in the area. Somehow Miss Paceley backed over a rock that took a plug out of the bottom of the gas tank. We frantically saved what gas we could in a thermos bottle and plugged the hole with chewing gum. We made it back to Taos where we had to spend the night. Another time we were heading to San Felipe, the next pueblo downstream from us on the Rio Grande, to go to church. It was a dark and stormy night. We were going fast and ran into a washout. I broke the windshield with my head and the fender was smashed. We walked into San Felipe for help. Miss Paceley was not what I'd call a skilled driver.

Not long after she bought her car Miss Paceley took little Maria with her into Domingo on the mail run. While there, the dog owned by the fellows who ran the Mercantile bit poor Maria on the leg. It wasn't a bad bite but Miss Paceley wanted to take her to see the nurse. Maria's father wouldn't hear of it. Instead he had Miss Paceley take him down to get some hairs off of the dog to put in the wound to cure it. He next wanted to kill the dog, but the owners shipped it off to Texas just in time. He might actually have done it too, since he was mad at us for not letting him use the school wheelbarrow. We wouldn't loan it to him anymore since the last time he'd borrowed it, he kept it for three months.

Adelido and Jose Garcia

The church bells in the village rang out frequently. They rang on Friday nights at the arrival of the weekend. They rang at other times to announce dances and other tribal festivities, when school was called off. Villagers would also travel to other pueblos to attend dances there. There were a few cars in the pueblo besides Miss Paceley's, but travel was usually by wagon or by walking to the highway and hitchhiking. It seemed like we seldom had a full week of school on account of a Saint's day or a dance or a rabbit hunt. At times the whites were allowed to observe the rituals. But if we dared to take a photograph, the camera would be taken away, the film yanked out and held up to the sun. Other times we were actually ordered to leave the Pueblo so we couldn't see the secret goings on. We were told to be gone "from sunup to sundown."

I was invited to participate in a rabbit hunt. These began in the early morning when a man all dressed up in bells ran to the top of the hill and called down to the village. Someone in the village would call back to him. This went on for some time but of course I couldn't understand what they were saying. Eventually the man left the hill, the

men left the village on horseback and the women on foot. Once outside of the village in the hunting area, the men on their horses chased the rabbits and shot them while the women on foot ran to retrieve the rabbits. The fastest women got the most rabbits. It was quite a sight to see fifty to seventy-five horsemen all close together, singing and chanting in their bright colored shirts and headbands returning to the village. The women with the rabbits, no longer on foot, followed in a dozen wagons. The next day the women would take a small basket of flour—one for each animal—to the men who had killed their rabbits. I would have gone if I could ride a horse but I surely wouldn't walk all that way and chase rabbits on foot.

Horseback riding was an activity I enjoyed in my spare time. Reyes or Monica or Joe or Tony would bring over their animals for us to use. Mostly they were plow horses that just plodded along, and were ancient history at that. Or they were untrained horses that would throw a person off at the least provocation. The Pueblos were among the first Indians to get horses from the Spanish in the 1600s. But being a settled, agricultural people, they did not take to the horse as readily as the Plains Indians to the north, who realized their value for hunting buffalo and other game. To the Pueblos, horses were mainly a trade item and eventually some were kept for farming and transportation.

The school year passed rapidly. We teachers took our first swim at our "private beach", a section of irrigation ditch, in early April but the water was still cold. The desert started coming to life with green grass

Dance I attended at Laguna Pueblo - late 1930s

sprouting all around. Some windmills for pumping water were installed in the village. This was an improvement in village life although it meant I wouldn't get as many visitors when they came up my way to haul water. Miss Perry graduated six children, all boys, from the sixth grade. From here they would go on to the Indian boarding school in Santa Fe, a big change for them. In Santa Fe the children would be mingling with students from all of the pueblos as well as Apaches and Navajos and others such as Utes, Cherokees, Pimas, and Kiowas.

As much as I loved New Mexico, it was pure joy to go home for a visit during summer vacation. Miss Paceley took me to the train depot in her car. After three weeks my mother, my twelve year old sister Ruth, and my two year old nephew, Dicky came back with me to stay for a few weeks. I had to secure permission from the Indian Council for their visit. Ruth took to Santo Domingo with relish. I bought Ruth her very first soda, a Nehi Orange, at the Mercantile. But coming from the land of fresh-squeezed orange juice, she thought the Nehi was awful! She explored the wide open country on horseback and befriended everyone. But my mother judged that I had taken up residence in a heathen country! She was appalled at my living conditions. Miss Paceley generously took all of us on trips to the Jemez Mountains and to other pueblos. It was really fun, sharing my experiences in the Indian country with my family members.

In mid-September 1935 I was back with my students in the classroom again. I was more confident about my teaching and more immersed in the village life. Often I would be invited to share a meal in someone's home. The homes were comfortable but sparse. Furnishings were usually a few old kitchen chairs and lots of blankets and bedrolls. Sometimes big sheets of linoleum were spread right on top of the hard-packed dirt. The meals were stew, usually goat or pork, with carrots and lots of chile, and bread or tortillas. Dinner was served in a big communal bowl on the floor into which we all dipped bread and tortillas.

The smallest things were such a treat to the kids. Pedro was elated over the new socks and the football his brother brought him from Albuquerque. He exclaimed about his football, "It cost 25 cents!" Delores was keeping me supplied with coal, two buckets for a piece of bread and butter with sugar on it. The time I offered her pickles on her bread instead she anxiously accepted, but the next day I found a neat little pile of green tomato pickles under the table. I guess she didn't know what pickles were, and when she found out she didn't like them.

My sister Ruth and friends

On the night of October 31st the village was illuminated by huge bon fires—the idea was to clean up trash and debris in preparation for the return of the ancestors on November 1st, All Souls Day. The next day there was a huge feast. The food was laid out in great style and the Indians talked to them as the ancestors "ate." Next the adult villagers actually did eat, and finally the children. The bell rang slowly all afternoon.

With Senor Tenorio's horses

School room and our house, Santo Domingo

Before Christmas I had my class put on a play of the Christmas Story. For the backdrop we painted murals of the Middle Eastern landscape, which really isn't so different from that of New Mexico. They did a beautiful job. Christmas Day brought hours of festivities and dances in the village despite the cold. Native dances took place amidst shrines of Mary and Jesus and long mumbled prayers in "Santo Domingo Latin." Dancers presented gifts "for the Christ Child" to the Governor and his Council.

January 6th was Reyes (Kings) Day commemorating the arrival of the Three Wise Men, and celebrated here in Santo Domingo with more feasting and dancing. Men and women both were dancers but only men were allowed to be the drummers. Again, school was canceled. In fact very few students had shown up at school that whole week. There was simply too much excitement going on.

Spring brought another lively event that I witnessed all three years that I taught at Santo Domingo. The grand ceremony celebrating the coming of the water down the ditch, which of course was used to water the crops, took place in March. The singing started at about three in the morning. I'm not sure if it was an official dance at that hour or if the men were just getting "in the mood" to work on the ditch the next morning. The school kids were excited and useless for studying. They stayed at the windows all morning until I let them out onto the playground. From there they seemed content to watch as the dancers ran out from the village one at a time followed by the women. Then they all gathered at the ditch—the men worked with their shovels on the ditch, the women sat on the ground in a colorful group furnishing the food. Occasionally three or four men would run up toward the village and be ceremoniously chased back again.

The ditch water came from the Rio Grande River. Most of the men did some farming. Chiles, a variety of short corn, beans, onions, pumpkins and squash seemed to be the main crops. In the fall, the chiles were brought into the houses in big heaps then strung up to dry. What a colorful, memorable sight—the adobe houses all festooned with bright red chiles hanging from the vegas.

That school year the children and I got a sad lesson. One day the Governor of the pueblo with ten of his officers came to school and told Miss Nori that he wanted to speak to all of the children about hanging on cars as they drove through the village. He also wanted to speak to several of the big boys who were misbehaving. We gathered on the floor in Miss Nori's room and Reyes interpreted. After the first message the Governor then said he was going to punish some boys but that we should not have any ill feeling toward him because he was doing what he knew to be right. He called up Adelido, Tony, Pedro, and Ramon. Ramon wasn't there so he substituted Vidal. He pulled out his three inch rawhide strap and gave them each a good horse whipping right in front of us. We were all aghast. Miss Nori stood right up and said she was going to immediately write up a report and send it to the main office, that this action was absolutely against regulations. The Governor was quite surprised that she would not

side with him. He left, glaring daggers.

Vidal was without a doubt the most outstanding boy in the school. His older brother came up and threatened to take him out of school, said he was good at home and if he was bad at school, well then he couldn't come to school anymore. After much talking we convinced him the punishment was none of our doing, that most likely Vidal was picked to be the fourth boy punished (when Ramon wasn't present) because he was squirming in his chair and caught the Governor's attention. The other boys had almost as little reason for punishment as far as we teachers knew. For Pedro there seemed to be no reason except that he came from a long line of lawbreakers. But shouldn't he be given a chance? Tony was a little rough but his father sometimes gave him liquor to drink. And Adelido was very good. But his father had an argument with the Governor over a horse in his cornfield. Adelido's father told the Governor he would shoot his horse if it got in his corn field

A gardening lesson

one more time. Well, next time it happened, his father gave Adelido the gun and told him to shoot the horse—which his obedient son did! So these village problems seemed to be getting settled in school. It was underhanded but I figured the Indians would take care of things in their own way and we were helpless to do much about it.

I heard from Mike Leva at the store about how one of the earliest white teachers, a Mr. Wiler, had been handled. Mike had been running the Mercantile for over twenty years so he knew the local people quite well. It seems Mr. Wiler went sneaking around the kiva, the circular house where the Indians held secret meetings and ceremonies, to see what was going on. Of course he got caught. Several weeks later (so the story goes) he completely lost his memory and his capacity to think clearly. Shortly after that he went to the insane asylum and it wasn't long before he died. Now Mike didn't say that the Indians did it, but....And Miss Nori said she believes they **could** do it, so...

On the tracks at Domingo Station

I made my long anticipated trip to Sweden in the summer of 1936, taking my mother to visit her mother, as well as her only sister and three brothers. What a delightful time we had! But that is another story.

I returned to Santo Domingo in September for the school year, my third year of teaching. I expected that I would stay in this job for a long time; I felt I was doing a good job. I liked the Santo Domingo Indians and they liked me. I was settling into this place. But in the Indian Service, we teachers went where we were told. And in the summer of 1937 I received an assignment that pleased me very much. My superiors decided that they would like me to have more first hand knowledge of some of the Indian crafts produced in the area. They arranged for me to spend time on the Pima and Papago Reservations learning about their local crafts, especially their fine basketry. I also stayed two weeks with Maria Martinez and her family at San Ildefonso Pueblo. San Ildefonso is a northern Pueblo and Tewa the native language.

Maria and her husband, Julian, were already well known not only for their beautiful pottery but also for helping to create a renaissance of Indian arts and crafts. Pueblo pottery is believed to have first been made around 500 AD. But pottery, and all the Indian arts, had sadly deteriorated with the growing misfortunes of the Pueblo culture. Tin and enamelware containers quickly replaced many of the handmade pots in Pueblo homes after the opening of the Santa Fe Trail in 1821.

Pottery recovered from archeological excavations on the Pajarito Plateau in the early 1900s aroused the interest of some of the San Ildefonso workmen. Dr. Edger Hewett, in charge of the excavation, and one of his associates, Mr. Kenneth Chapman of the School of American Research induced Maria and Julian in San Ildefonso, and later Monica Silva in Santo Domingo to make pottery using traditional methods and designs. There began a newly awakened interest in ceramics in the pueblos. This happily led to some commercial success, which in turn led to more technical and artistic excellence. Maria and Julian were leaders of this movement.

In their partnership Maria made the pots and Julian decorated them. Unlike most Pueblo men he did not farm. In the early years he worked for wages wherever he could, such as for the railroad. He also worked for some years at the Santa Fe Museum and at various archeological digs, so he had been exposed to large quantities of pottery from many different sources. Painting Maria's pots became Julian's vocation. Julian incorporated designs from other places into his decorations, not only traditional San Ildefonso designs.

What an exciting opportunity for me. I would be able to learn more about this craft, get to know Maria and Julian better and to visit another pueblo for a time. I had first met Marie (as I called her) and Julian at the Palace of Governors in Santa Fe where they often went to sell pottery on Saturdays. Now I moved right into the Martinez home. Like everyone else, they lived in a flat roofed adobe home, but it sat on a hill a little away from the others. There were low benches and lots of blankets rolled up on the floor. There was a corner fireplace for heat and a wood stove for cooking.

Shortly after my arrival Marie's daughter-in-law Santana, who later worked with Maria, gave birth right there in her adobe house. I'll never forget it. Early in the morning Marie and I walked down the hill together to Santana's house in the village. She was lying on the floor in the corner of the room. The famous hands that molded clay into priceless pots skillfully carried out the duties of midwife, and little Sunset came into the world.

In those two weeks, I worked with Marie every step of the way and made a few pots of my own. The first step was to collect the clay. We walked for miles to the pits. She pulled out a small pouch of cornmeal and sprinkled it over the earth in a blessing for its gifts. We brought the clay home in baskets, then ground it and mixed it with sand and water.

Marie made the pots in a variety of shapes, starting with a pancake of clay supported on a

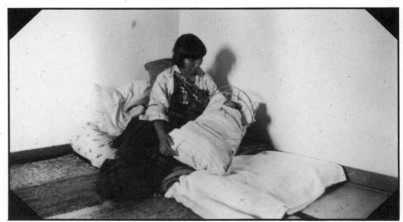

Santana with Sunset

puki just the right size. From there on the clay was added in coils then thinned and smoothed into shape. Her sister Clara, who was mute, polished the pots with rocks. Next Julian painted the decorative bands with a yucca brush dipped in clay slip (clay mixed with water to a cream-like consistency). Then the pots were dried in the hot sun.

Finally the pots were fired. To do this the pots were placed on top of a wood fire and the whole thing was covered with dried cow dung patties. When the pots were well-baked, the whole mound was completely covered and smothered with a fine, pulverized manure. The fire would smolder for hours. This caused the pots to turn a beautiful black, the famous blackware which is now recognized as typically "San Ildefonso." Neighboring Santa Clara Pueblo is also known for its black pottery.

Marie was very worldly for a person born in an isolated pueblo in the previous century. She was born in 1887 and became interested in pottery at a young age by watching her Aunt Nicolasa shape pots. Her aunt was one of the few remaining traditional potters at that time. Indian potters never invented and still seldom use a potter's wheel. All of the pottery produced at that time was polychrome decorated in two or more colors. The famous blackware came later. The pots were not for sale. They were made for household use or trading only, for mixing or cooking or collecting rain water.

Marie coiled her first pot at about age seven or eight. She

had gained a reputation as a skilled potter by the time of her marriage at age 17 to Julian in 1904. They spent their honeymoon that summer performing dances at the World's Fair in St. Louis, where Marie also made pots in front of the crowds. It was the first of several world's fairs and other travels that would take her all over the country in the following decades as she became famous.

So when Mr. Chapman and Dr. Hewett were intrigued by the shiny black potsherds that had been found in the excavations on the Pajarito Plateau in 1908 and 1909, they went to Maria. They were looking for a local Indian woman (for traditionally only women were potters) to make pots the way she thought the pieces would look if they were whole. It was the beginning of the famous San Ildefonso black pottery. She had no trouble making the pots true to form, but why the clay turned black in the firing was something of a mystery. Julian did some experimenting and discovered that it was best to fire on an absolutely calm day and that smothering the fire to deprive it of oxygen, produced the blackware.

With encouragement from the learned men the couple perfected their techniques. Marie learned how to achieve the beautiful luster and smooth finish by long polishing with a round stone. The artistic Julian began to paint designs on Marie's pots with clay slip after the polishing was done. The painted designs came out of the firing with a matte finish that contrasted with the shiny black surface, and so the black-on-black ware came to be. The first pieces, and hundreds thereafter, were decorated with *avanyu* designs, the horned water serpent, a symbol of thanksgiving for rain and water.

The prices they received for their works in the early days were astonishingly small, a dollar or two a pot, yet they were able to support the family with their craft. Marie was community and family-oriented despite her unusual success and growing fame. She generously shared her techniques with family and friends. Over the years she worked with sisters Clara, Anna, brother-in-law Crescencio, daughter-in-law Santana, and sons Adam and Popovi Da. Others from San Ildefonso learned the craft. A new measure of pride and economical success developed in the community. She became the matriarch of five generations of potters.

I was intrigued with the whole pottery-making process, that summer of 1937. It seemed to me something I should share with my students. I took photos of everything and in my spare time wrote a story for my second and third graders. I pasted up a modest little book thinking to use it during the next school year. Little did I know that the Indian Service and destiny had other plans for me. Now, sixty years later, I am finally presenting that book to my students!

My orders were to transfer to the Indian School in Santa Fe. My official title would be Teacher of Fine and Applied Arts. I was thrilled at the opportunity to become more involved in the art world but sad to be leaving Santo Domingo. It seems I had made some friends, because the Governor and his Council came to me and asked me not to leave. I calmed them by explaining that I would now be teaching the children of Santo Domingo when they went on to the boarding school, that I would be there to keep a watchful eye and help them make the transition.

Moving to Santa Fe was a transition for me as well, although not as much as the change from La Verne, California to Santa Domingo, New Mexico. I now lived in a faculty dormitory with plenty of hot water and no blowing sand and ate with the others in a dining hall. My work there involved much more than teaching. It was a test of my organizational skills. The next four years were a busy time for me.

I was in charge of the entire Arts and Crafts Department with ten people working under me. Some of the best native artisans were employed as teachers for the high school students. We had instructors of woodworking (George Pacheco, later known as Blue Spruce, from Laguna Pueblo), painting (Jerry Montoya from San Juan Pueblo), silversmithing (Ambrose Roanhorse and Wilfred Jones, who were Navajos), leathercraft and tanning

Santa Fe Indian School office

(Reyes Durant from Taos), weaving and embroidery (Lucy Lowden from Jemez Pueblo.) We had a sales and display room. Enough quality work was created to send off exhibits to museums, universities, fairs, and ceremonials around the country.

One of my favorite projects included several Santo Domingo boys who were silversmith students. They did very well making the Navajo-style jewelry that tourists loved. But they wanted to make something different, something using designs from their own cultural background. So we consulted Mr. Chapman's book, *The Pottery of Santo Domingo*, to come up with authentic designs. The possibilities were many and the boys were enthusiastic. Tony Aguilar, a boy I had known in Santo Domingo, was one of the prize students. Soon Tony and the others were making steel

stamps of the Santo Domingo designs I had drawn from Mr. Chapman's book and combining them in a variety of ways with the help of their instructor, Wilfred Jones. Mr. Chapman himself visited the workshop and was splendid about giving suggestions and constructive criticism from time to time.

Within a few months we had enough authentic Santo Domingo silver jewelry to exhibit at the Inter-Tribal Ceremonial in Gallup. They won the blue ribbon and got a request to exhibit at the New York Museum of Fine Art.

Naturally the boys were very encouraged by all of the recognition and inspired to continue with their work. Tony has spent all of his life crafting this beautiful authentic jewelry. The two of us have kept in touch throughout the years.

For several months while stationed at the Santa Fe Indian School, I had the interesting experience of working with Rene d'Harnoucourt who was in charge of the Indian Arts and Crafts Board in Washington D.C.. I traveled with him to the different pueblos collecting items to be exhibited at the World's Fair on Treasure Island, San Francisco in 1939-1940. The fair was to celebrate the opening of the new Golden Gate and Bay Bridges, in a world very far removed from the pueblos of New Mexico.

Santa Domingo silversmith students in Santa Fe workshop - 1940

Tony Aguilar, Mr. Kenneth Chapman and Mr. Wilford Jones planning jewelery design stamps, Santa Fe Indian School - 1940

Apparently the Bureau of Indian Affairs felt that my work in Santa Fe was complete after about four years, even if I didn't. I was ordered to transfer to Browning, Montana as soon as possible. According to my orders, "The most direct route should be followed (consult Indian Service Route Book.)" Like every other American alive at that time, I remember well Pearl Harbor Day, Dec. 7, 1941. I was still in Santa Fe, but two days later I was in the Oldsmobile I'd purchased while in Santa Fe driving to Montana by myself. It was a sad parting. I had made so many friends and learned so much in my nearly six years in New Mexico.

I was given a similar job at the newly opened Museum of the Plains Indian in Browning just outside Glacier National Park. But I was no longer involved with teaching. My new job title was "Arts and Crafts Marketing Specialist" and I was now making $2000 a year working with adult Indians rather than young students.

Whereas the Pueblo Indians of New Mexico had always been relatively peaceful, nonaggressive farmers, these Indians of the high plains in Montana had to make a much greater transition to reservation life after their way of life was turned upside down by white people. The Plains Indians had been militant buffalo hunters. But the buffalo disappeared, thanks to non-Indian hunters and the coming of the railroad, by the mid-1880s, leaving hundreds of Indians to starve before the United States government stepped in.

In the early 1940s when I worked in Browning there were still a few Indians alive who had strong, happy memories of when their people had been the masters of their region. These elderly men and women had been born in teepees, raised with the ancient religious beliefs, learned the traditional arts, hunted buffalo from horseback, raided horses from enemy tribes.

I worked with Plains Indian tribes on eight reservations in Montana and Wyoming including the Blackfoot, Fort Belknap, Rocky Boy, and Wind River Reservations. My job was to organize artist's cooperatives complete with bylaws and constitutions to enable the far-flung tribes to market their crafts. Things were disorganized and there was some tension and apathy among my fellow workers. I could see I had a big job ahead of me. I grew discouraged at times.

During the first few months after arriving in Browning, I enjoyed traveling around the various Plains Indian reservations with Mable

Blackfeet in front of the Museum of the Plains Indian, Browning -1942

Venerable Plains Indian In Montana

Marrow, specialist in Arts and Crafts from the Bureau of Indian Affairs, Washington D.C. She was a unique individual, well-versed in Indian culture. I was very fortunate to have Miss Marrow to introduce me to the diverse Plains tribes and to help get me acclimated to my new environment. She later went on to author the book *Indian Rawhide.*

The reservations were quite spread out but I liked traveling around the countryside in my government car. I named that car Pearl, short for Pearl Harbor, because it was "shot to pieces," although it did get me everywhere I needed to go. My contacts were mainly the teachers in the reservation schools, who knew the local artists. One of the teachers would go with me to talk to the craftsmen. I would tell them about the cooperative and place orders for their work. My duties were many and included bookkeeping and even wrapping and shipping orders. I ordered the needed raw materials but often didn't receive them due to war time scarcities. We were trying to develop a strong market for the Indian crafts, but at the same time many Indians were drifting into the war industries.

Now my sister Ruth was in college. She visited me in Browning but considered it "a hole in the wall." Still, we were both ceremoniously adopted into the Blackfoot tribe. Ruth was given the name Yellow Owl Woman and I was Pretty Star Woman. The reservation homes were mostly run down wooden shacks, but they all seemed to own automobiles, unlike the Pueblo Indians.

One of the biggest events of the summer season was the annual sun dance that took place on July 4th. The sun dance camp was set up between the Museum and the Agency Hospital. The thirty or so teepees bore traditional symbolic paintings and were arranged in a circle around the medicine lodge. Each year the sun dance was initiated by a woman who took on the

Sundance encampment, July 4th

responsibility in return for the sun's protection for an ill or dying family member. During the war years, protection was sought for the many young Indian men serving in the military.

The sun dance lasted four days. It was a long, complicated ceremony but the old man who was the director of the dance knew all the proper prayers, songs, and movements. Old men chanted and beat on buffalo hide drums, young men dancers faced the sun and blew into eagle bone whistles, warriors hung offerings to the sun on the medicine lodge poles, stories were told, songs sung. It was a ritual for renewal, the major religious ceremony of the Blackfeet, a colorful and unforgettable event for me to witness.

In 1943 I became good friends with artist Winold Reiss who was in Browning that summer to continue his lifelong passion: drawing and painting the Indian portraits for which he became famous. His study trips to Montana began in 1919. The trips were paid for by the Great Northern Railroad who commissioned his Indian portraits for their brochures and calendars. That summer he set up his studio in the Yegan Hotel. His easel was bathed in the natural light of a window, his subjects sat at a table opposite him and were entertained by a younger Indian hired to tell legends to keep them relaxed. Winold produced seventy-five more portraits that summer. No wonder the Indians gave him the name Beaver Man—he was a diligent worker.

I now earned $3021 a year. I enjoyed my work but I never felt quite as at home in Montana as I had in New Mexico. And in any case, the world was changing, our country was at war. In a patriotic urge, I joined the WAVES, the United States Naval Reserve, in the summer of 1944. I drove

My domicile in Browning

Wolf Child by Winold Reiss , Cree Indian from Rocky Boy Reservation

home to California for a quick visit. Too soon, my father walked me down to the corner to catch the bus into Los Angeles. That was the last time I ever saw him alive. From Los Angeles a whole train full of recruits headed east for New York. There were no sleepers. We sat up for days and were black and grimy with soot by the time we got there.

My time in the Navy was spent at St. Albans Hospital in Long Island, New York. I worked in the Occupational Therapy Department instructing injured servicemen in weaving, woodworking, printing, cord-knotting, leather work, chip carving, and bookbinding. While in New York, my father died and I returned home to help Mother. I was given a Hardship Discharge with full veteran's benefits. Now I was able to do some postgraduate work. While taking a class at Scripps College in Claremont, California, I met Sam, who was working for painter Millard Sheets, and within a few months we began our life together.

Marie and I kept up our friendship and exchanged visits throughout the decades. It was sixty years ago that I lived in New Mexico. But I still hold the country and the people close to my heart.

St. Albans Hospital, New York -1943

Maria Martinez Makes Pottery

Maria walked many miles
to find the clay.
Maria grinds the clay.
She grinds the clay until
it is very fine like powder.

Maria mixes the clay with sand.
She adds a little water to the mixed
clay to make it wet.
The wet clay looks like dough.

Maria first makes
a little round flat base.

She rolls out a coil of clay and
pinches it onto the little round base.

Maria adds another coil of clay.

She builds the pot higher and higher.

Maria shapes the pots
with her hands.

She uses a piece of gourd

to shape the pots.

Little pots. Big pots.

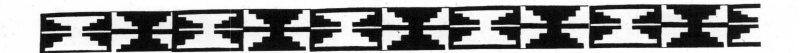

Maria's sister Clara

helps polish the pots.

Maria's husband Julian

decorates the pots.

Maria has finished her pottery.

The pottery has been polished.

Polished with little rocks.

The pottery has been decorated.

Decorated with a yucca brush

dipped in soft clay.

The pottery has been dried.

Dried in the hot sun

for many, many days.

Now it is time to fire the pots.

Maria puts the pots close together
on an old iron grate.

Julian helps Maria

fire the pots.

They place pieces of flat tin

around the pots

and on top of the pots.

They cover the whole thing

with cakes of manure.

Julian has set fire

to the small pieces of wood

under the pots.

Now the fire is burning.

The fire burns and burns

for many hours.

The pots get very hot.

The fire is cooking the clay.

Maria and Julian wait all day
while the fire burns
and bakes the clay.

Maria wants black pots.
So they pour manure dust
over the pottery oven.

The manure will smother the fire.

It will make a thick smoke.

The pots will change from red

to black.

Now it is time to take the pots
out of the hand-made oven.
The pots are too hot to touch.
Maria and Julian
poke carefully in the ashes
with long sticks.

They lift the hot pots out of the ashes
with the sticks so they will not
burn their hands.

Now Maria's pottery is finished.

All the pots are out of the fire.

Many, many pots.

Hot black pots.

Beautiful pots!

BIBLIOGRAPHY

Bunzel, Ruth L. *The Pueblo Potter, A Study of Creative Imagination in Primitive Art.* Dover Publications, Inc., New York, 1932.

The Indians. Time-Life Books, New York, 1973.

Chapman, Kenneth M. *The Pottery of Santo Domingo Pueblo, A Detailed Study of Its Decoration,* Laboratory of Anthropology, Santa Fe, New Mexico, 1936

Maloof, Alfreda Ward. Personal papers, photo albums, diaries.

Peterson, Susan. *The Living Tradition of Maria Martinez.* Kodansha International/USA Ltd., New York, 1989.

Sides, Dorothy Smith. *Decorative Art of the Southwestern Indians.* Dover Publications, Inc., New York, 1961.

Stewart, Jeffrey C. *To Color America, Portraits by Winold Reiss.* Smithsonian Institution Press, Washington City, 1989.

Spivey, Richard L. *Maria.* Northland Press, Flagstaff, Arizona, 1979.

With Santana and Adam Martinez, San Ildefonso - 1996

To order additional copies of

Recollections from My Time in the Indian Service 1935-1943 ◆ Maria Martinez Makes Pottery

please send:

$15.00 plus $2.50 shipping and handling

(CA residents add $1.08 sales tax)

to

LIVING GOLD PRESS

P.O. Box 2
Klamath River, CA 96050